THE RECREATED Woman

How to Incorporate God's Plan Into Your Life

TABITHA HENTON LAMB

Copyright © 2023 Tabitha Henton Lamb.

ISBN: 978-969-3992-22-9 Paperback
ISBN: 978-969-3992-21-2 eBook

All rights reserved. No part of this book may be reproduced, stored, or transmitted by any means—whether auditory, graphic, mechanical, or electronic—without written permission of both publisher and author, except in the case of brief excerpts used in critical articles and reviews. Unauthorized reproduction of any part of this work is illegal and is punishable by law.

The scriptures quoted in this book are taken from the King James Version. The King James Version is in the public domain unless otherwise noted.

Please note that KJV has no quote marks when someone is speaking

Contents

Introduction v

Chapter 1 God's Original Intent 1
Chapter 2 Identity 9
Chapter 3 Security in God 17
Chapter 4 Submission versus Subjection 25
Chapter 5 The Power of Influence 35
Chapter 6 The Spirit of Seduction 49
Chapter 7 The Contentious Woman 61
Chapter 8 The Virtuous Woman 71
Chapter 9 God's Revelations to Women 77

Commitment Pledge 99
Notes 101

Introduction

The Women's Rights Movement since the 1960's has made great strides in enforcing our rights and removing discrimination. This progress is to be commended. And yet so many women still go through continuing disparity and hardship, and great sorrows continue to be heaped upon them. The main issues are revealed in the Garden. This is the root of our problem. This is where our success in the Women's Rights Movement has failed us. Until we deal with it here, we will continue in disparity and hardship. What is our remedy for this?

You see, the problem comes in our relationship with God, with men and with our children. This is the hand dealt us as a result of a decision the first woman, standing, as it were, in proxy for all womankind. But God wants us to know the total remedy is in Him; it is only through Jesus that the root cause can be completely destroyed.

This book reveals how much we are loved and cherished by God in spite of our errors. He has made a way for us to find ourselves again. Although Eve made a wrong decision, God still covered and protected her by providing a redemption plan, partly because of her and for the generations after her. He provided proper garments to protect her in her newfound environment apart from Him. Most importantly, He gave her the promise of redemption, which has been fulfilled in Jesus, the promised seed of the woman.

This book reveals the nature of this newly established woman that exists apart from the original design for her. All of our issues began with her choice as they do with our own choices. The word of God reveals in detail the kind of "women" we evolved into as a result. The character and nature of this new woman is clearly revealed in scripture for us to receive and to learn from. The onus is on us to identify what is our God-given nature according to the word of God and not what we believe to be true of ourselves. Although we want to be seen as good, there is an opposing nature in us that we must come face to face with. This is the key to changing the circumstances of our lives.

The truth is, God has a wonderful plan for us, but we have rejected it and followed our own plan. We must now make the exchange in Him to receive it. We must look at the character and design of the world's version of the "woman" and the role she has been assigned. The serpent handed out seduction and Eve operated in that same spirit. We must look closely at this spirit to see how it contrasts with God's perspective in the word of God, not only in the fruit produced in our own lives but also in society.

Jesus is our remedy as He is our promise. If we seek to break the neck of this enemy, we must recognize that he is a deceiver, so we must begin with the truth. We must clearly identify where we went wrong and make a sound decision according to the knowledge received. This is the substance of this book.

We start with our identity in Christ. If you've never had a true father figure in your life, learn how God honors us through the life of Jesus and His encounters with us. This can be your point of reference if you will believe in Him. This book is all about the biblical principles laid out to us by God. These truths will guard us against the female stereotypes fabricated and often forced upon us by our postmodern culture.

While we as women all seek security, unfortunately, more often than not, we end up with the exact opposite. This place of true security that we earnestly seek is ultimately in God alone. It is not until we are secure in Him that we can come to a state of security in the world around us.

The chapter on submission shows our God-given purpose, and distinguishes it from subjection. However, the prospect of surrendering our will to another can seem like a terrifying prospect without Him. For some of us it is just that. If we go back to the beginning to understand why God created us and His purpose for our existence, submission takes on an entirely different tone.

And finally, the chapter on God's Revelations to Women reveals His heart and intent through the words, the deeds, the tenderness, and the compassion of Jesus – how He handled her and how He revealed Himself to her. Even if her culture sees her as inferior or irrelevant, know that God shared some of the most powerful revelations to her and she became His greatest witness. If you look at scriptures you will see that women were used as the witnesses to the announcement and revealing of His coming in human flesh. That He was the Messiah was revealed to women, that He was the resurrection and life was affirmed through a woman, and finally that the risen Christ was first revealed to a woman.

Chapter 1

God's Original Intent

Adam had purpose, occupation, responsibility and a home even before Eve appeared. One of Adam's responsibilities was to name every living creature; this was no small task because it meant understanding their characteristics and dividing them into genus, species and sub species. But it became clear that Adam needed a helper that would "correspond" to him. The Lord knew this and said, "It is not good that the man should be alone: and based on this assessment He said, I will make him an help meet for him" (Genesis 2:18, 20). So "He caused a deep sleep to fall upon Adam, and he slept: and he took one of his ribs, and closed up the flesh thereof; And the rib, He took from the man, He made a woman, and brought her unto the man" (Genesis 2:21-22). The woman was all that was required to complement Adam. She was designed to be the solution to man's loneliness and his perfect companion.

Through this act, God made it clear that He did not need man's help and to prevent the man from taking credit for this development. Adam's response to what God made for him was, "This is now bone of my bone, and flesh of my flesh: she shall be called Woman because she was taken out of man." The Bible then says, "Therefore shall a man leave his father and his mother, and shall cleave unto his wife: and they shall be **one flesh**" (Genesis 2:24).

Both the first man and woman were created in God's likeness and given dominion over every living thing:

> And God said, Let us make man in our image, after our likeness: and let them have dominion over the fish of the sea, and over the fowl of the air, and over the cattle, and over all the earth, and over every creeping thing that creepeth upon the earth. So God created man in his own image, in the image of God created he him; male and female created he them. And God blessed them, and God said unto them, Be fruitful, and multiply, and replenish the earth, and subdue it: and have dominion over the fish of the sea, and over

the fowl of the air, and over every living thing that moveth upon the earth (Genesis 1:26-28).

The above verses are profound. To find fulfillment in the life that we seek, we must go back to the original intent of God. He created each human being with purpose, both for the woman as it is for the man. Whether or not we are willing to accept this truth, it is still an objective reality apart from us. Are we on the same quest as Eve to stake our own claim to our own identity as distinct from God's plan? Why is the purpose and plan of God for woman not enough?

Now this is worth contemplating. At her creation, the first person that Eve set her eyes upon was Father God. How marvelous for her to see her Creator in all His majesty! How wonderful to see His delight in her! There is nothing further conveyed about this introduction but the first eyes that she saw and the first touch she felt were from her Father.

The Bible says that He presented her to the man, but only after a home had been prepared and furnished with provision for her. Then the command to be fruitful came. This is what my own journey has shown me. In my personal quest for God and His will for my life, it has brought me face to face with Father God. I can finally see His love, His security, His provision, His protection. I have encountered Jesus and communed with Holy

Spirit. It is how I have been introduced to the Father: in this I am one with Him, by Him and through Him.

So God fashioned Eve and positioned her to be the glory of Adam. She was his – not to be ruled by him, controlled by him, manipulated or dominated by him – but to be loved and cherished by him, to be covered, to be protected. God gave her a representation of Himself in the person of Adam, in a visible, tangible form, in flesh and blood. God would take the time to form a version of Him but a softer form with a womb and reproductive organs. She was designed for Adam. I can only imagine the beauty in and upon her, the glory of God in likeness and form.

Think about it. God could have allowed Adam to be the first one for Eve to set her eyes upon; but He did not. What a message to us women! When He fashioned Adam alone, separate and apart and then Eve, was He not conveying to her the following: "Even though I formed you for him, you are Mine, separate and apart from him"? My dear sisters, this is what He wants us to know. "Even though Adam has gone against Me, you are still Mine. He went astray partly because of you in misusing your power of influence. Nevertheless, you are still beloved in My eyes and I call you Mine."

The woman is the crown of her husband, fearfully and meticulously made, fashioned intentionally for man. She was made on purpose with a purpose – from a rib taken from the side of Adam in that he is complete with a part of him outside of himself.

God's Original Intent

So God took her out of Adam and formed her for him. Did the serpent oppose this union in tempting her to see herself apart from her husband as her own entity or god? Why are our men not equipped to handle this aspect of woman? Is it because they have received the wrong teaching concerning her? Is this what has aided in the violent treatment and abuse towards the woman? We must also return back to the original intent by God for her to put away any misconception of her and arm herself with the truth about herself.

So He gave the woman reproductive organs to bear children. We agree with this truth. We accept it and abide by it. Why then is there this inner disdain for the act of submission? Did Eve think she would gain something more by being equal to Adam in terms of the role given him by God? Yes, she was equal in terms of her standing with God; but she was functionally under her husband when it came to authority. This follows the divine pattern shown by God. Even though Jesus was equal with the Father (Philippians 2:5), He submitted to the will of the Father in all things (Philippians 2:8; John 5:19; Luke 22:42).

It is out of the distorted thinking that submission is part of the curse that the "women's rights movement" was birthed. Are we seeking to do away with the assigned role of Eve? We find it hard and grievous to submit because it is now perceived as a curse and not a blessing for us. But Jesus broke the curse of subjection and liberated the woman's seed by making Himself subject to the law and bearing the brunt of it for us. In Him, we are therefore restored and able to enjoy all of the fruits of marriage in submission to Him and to one another. However, we cannot be unequally yoked with an unbeliever and claim this promise. We must wait on God to bring us the right man and stop searching and seeking out our own man. The Bible says that he that finds a wife finds a good thing and obtains the favor of God. This reveals we are to be hidden and not on public display. You may ask hidden where? Hidden in Christ. If we truly seek Him first, He will add all that is required for both our pleasure and well-being; but we must seek it in Him and not apart from Him.

In essence, a woman does not belong to herself. She was not formed from her own parts but from the rib of man. Why? Because it was not good for man to be alone. We are the complement from God to him. Why is this not enough for us? Is it our quest to be our own independent self when our true purpose is to complement the man? This also explains the man in his search for her as he is looking for the part outside of himself. She is, in fact, so much an integral part of him that if he mistreats her, he is mistreating himself.

We are the glory of the man – a crown unto our husband, the rib removed from the side of Adam. Like the side of Jesus pierced for His church, when He gave Himself for her, how much more should man give himself for the other part of himself, for the total complete well-being of himself!

This question brought all sorts of emotional reactions to me personally. Why is the purpose of God for woman not enough? It immediately took me back to my questions to Him as a little girl. "God," I asked, "why does it seem like the woman is mistreated by the man, and it seems to be okay and goes unpunished?" You see, when I was young, I would read the Bible and always notice the many stories of how the women were ill-treated and mishandled by the men of the Bible. Think of Lot, for example, when he offered to hand over his daughters to the perverted men at the door to do as they wished with them with no regard to how they would be harmed or damaged. We are back to the same question of submission. For me, the very thought of me having to trust this kind of callous unfeeling man brought shudders to me. The idea of giving myself to such a person in this way seemed so reckless. It seemed like I was asking for a repeated cycle of pain and suffering.

It appeared to be the revealing of another area God wanted in me. This is what brought me to the point of taking a step back to identify the true purpose of the plan of God for the woman. It may be easier to identify with the plan of God rather than conceive of the idea of surrendering myself to a man who appeared so irresponsible. However, I had to choose to put myself completely in His will to understand His total plan for me.

This led me to a place of wanting to know my true identity and to be secure in it.

Chapter 2

Identity

In the previous chapter we talked about submission and authority. We are now going to go back to the beginning to properly identify and define who God framed the woman to be. If her purpose was decided before she was formed, then should we not frame our reality around this?

Let us first define identity. Identity is the state or quality of being at once the same or unique. This is powerful. God made Eve the same as Adam and they were of the same substance. However, He made Eve unique in essence and nature.

The Godhead decided to make the human race man and woman as partners. Not a woman outside or apart from man but from him. Elohim decided, "We are going to make him in our image and after Our likeness. The very essence of who We are is to be embodied in the flesh to rule over the earth and over all things created. We are going to give them dominion over the works of Our hands." In saying "let them …" Elohim conveyed their assignment and authority to rule over all of the earth and all things upon the earth on His behalf. What an amazing mission for a creature made of dust! Psalm 8 describes the wonder of it all:

What is man, that thou art mindful of him? and the son of man, that thou visitest him? For thou hast made him a little lower than the angels, and hast crowned him with glory and honour. Thou madest him to have dominion over the works of thy hands; thou hast put all things under his feet … (Psalm 8:4-6)

So the triune God created man according to Their agreed collaboration: male and female. Then He blessed them to carry out His plan of creation for humanity, the earth and all upon it. Let me rephrase these instructions in my own way: "Here is how it will manifest itself as long as you carry it out. Be fruitful, producing good or helpful results; be productive. Multiply, to increase or to make more in number, quantity or degree. Replenish, fill up something again, to restore to a former level of condition. Subdue the earth, overcome it, quell it, bring it under control. Exercise dominion, the power or right of governing or controlling through My sovereign authority."

Therefore, in order to effectively deal with our identity issues, we must first define woman the way God intended her to be. We must define who He created her to be and why – that implies her

Identity

being, her role and job description on earth. He created humankind to be like Him in essence, in nature and in character. What did He have in mind when He created her? He took her from the side of man under His heart to be loved and cherished by him. She was to rule and have dominion with him – not separate or apart from him – but as one, to rule from under his arm, as it were, as her protector. This is absolutely beautiful and what I believe to be the true desire of every woman.

The crosswire is, do we see ourselves the way God sees us? How do we do that when all we know is what we have been socialized to be? This was my prayer to Him. It is here that the renewal of the mind is so imperative. We must put on the right truth and let go of what has improperly defined us. God's measure is a much higher measure and quality of life than we presently experience. It is a standard apart from this world, or what the world defines as a woman. Unless we begin here, it will be difficult to come into true purpose of who we are.

We are a product of our culture, our environment and ultimately our choices, and how we are reared. In spite of all of this, we are fundamentally the product of our DNA, that is, who God created us to be, and we must get to this place of being in our mind. The Father presented Eve as a crown unto her husband, beloved by him and beloved by God. He presented her as a Father presents his daughter in marriage to convey all of the words only a true father would say to the man: provide for her, protect her, love her, cover her, be a husband to her, and a covering for her frailties. This is the position Eve moved away from when she made her own choice.

But Eve made the decision to place her security outside of the godly covering of her husband. This happened before the fall, not as a result of it. She did not consider Adam and nor did she consult with him. This was absolute disrespect to him and to the role he was to play in her life. This also disrespected the role she was to position herself in before God. She rejected all he was to her and decided to make her own choice and her own way. She would now be responsible for herself outside of him – and that meant removing herself from his covering, his protection, his guidance, his instructions, wisdom and guidance.

We resemble her more now than in any previous generation. The woman wants nothing to do with the man's assigned role in relation to her. This stems partly because of the disparity she experiences in male's treatment of her due to the stereotyping of the female gender. But could it also be due to her attempt to break the perceived curse of seeing herself subject to man in her own strength?

The Seal of Insecurity

With our lost or ambivalent identity, women are faced with the seal of insecurity. We have no firm concept of where we belong and our self-concept keeps shifting.

I remember during prayer, the Lord revealed to me I had an issue with identity. He took me back to a certain place and time where an episode transpired. Words were spoken over me that crushed my heart and spirit. I remember those words vividly and I also remember coming into agreement with them. The Lord literally walked me through the corridor of this pain in my heart – but not until I was able to handle it. He held my hand as He shone the light upon my issue and revealed the truth. I did not feell any fear whatsoever. He guided me and He took me all the way back to the entry point of that pain; then He held that moment up to the light and healed me. He identified what it was that happened to me and He allowed me to see what I exchanged and what I accepted from the spoken words.

You see, the enemy had used a certain person to tear me down and to take away a certain belief in myself that God had put inside of me. But God allowed me to see how the enemy was trying to break me so that I would not come into my God-given purpose. God went in and uprooted the seed and all that came with it.

For the first time in my life I can say I am living and enjoying a truly fulfilling life, a life filled with the liberty of God in and through Christ Jesus. How amazing and beautiful to be free!! I had been fighting in my own strength against the seed of the enemy that was planted on the inside of me through words. But God took that seed away. This is what it was all about – the need to go back and to reclaim what was there. He is so good. He came for it all. He is better than life itself and there is no real or true life outside of Him. He wants to give this to all of us. He allows us to be opened, not for further damage, but so He can heal and restore us.

My sister, there is safety in all of the storms in this life when we realize they are allowed by God and ordained for growth. Sometimes we can be so consumed with the notion of safety and trying to find a place to hide that it can hinder God's ordained growth in our lives. Growth often comes through exposure to evil. But He is the kind of God we can trust with our innermost parts. We can see ourselves so clearly when He speaks. He is after the real person and that includes all the good as well as all the tarnished parts. The truth sets us free. He reveals things about us. He reveals answers to questions. Because we are safe in Him, there is no need to hide when you are in the midst of true love. We do not have to be afraid to be open or to be naked with Him.

We must break the cycle of insecurity in our lives. These insecurities are often ones that define us according to the world's description of a woman. This is the seal that must be broken in

Identity

our hearts and minds: the seal of our culture, our upbringing, and this world's stamp of its kind of woman. Rather, we must define who we are according to what the word of God has to say about the woman as God designed her to be and why. So our basic insecurity is something we must confront.

In my younger life I was heavy into modeling. This is a very competitive and lucrative business – I mean you can earn a week's salary in just a few hours. The fashion industry is always looking for the "new look" for what has not been captured or featured. This season could be all about the eyes, the next about the cheekbone or lips, just whatever they want to capitalize on. The ladies would go out and binge because they could not be over a size 0 or a size 2. They would starve themselves if for some reason they were not chosen. It was personal to them. Due to this exposure, I had to learn early on that I could not make it a personal thing. If I was not what they were looking for, it simply meant I did not fit the criteria. After all, not everybody can be a ballerina or opera singer! However, many of my peers would go out and have these surgeries to meet the expectation and then it would change in the next season. This is how fads and trends work, whereas we go and do things to our bodies that are permanent.

This is definitely not an industry for young impressionable girls, although they are often the innocent target – the lens has a way of capturing it. If by chance a certain girl was chosen, she was perfect for the moment and the rest of the population was not, that is, until she realized that her time was short-lived, and she was replaced with the next "new." In this law of the jungle, it was imperative to find a happy medium: to be happy and humble whether you were chosen or not; if not, to shrug it off as just not my season. This would give us the maturity to celebrate others in their season and not to walk away with resentment or see it as another blow to our self-concept.

I also realized that modeling was not an industry for morality or ethics. The more you were willing to take off, the more lucrative the pay. This gave me quite a bit of experience with women and how unkindly they sometimes treat one another. There is nothing more beautiful than a woman who is secure in her identity to the degree she can celebrate and rejoice with another over her victory. It is not about what she has, or what she has accomplished, or who she married. Neither is it about how well shaped she is. It is the quality of her inner life: this is what makes her beautiful. Her heart-life is in the right order towards God. This woman is graced by Him with a beauty that is bestowed upon her, for He beautifies the meek. True beauty is the quality of a person.

But of course, the world's definition of beauty is that which gives pleasure to the senses by a combination of shape, color or form, all set to please the esthetic senses, especially sight. This is too unstable to put one's security in. So where do we put our security?

Chapter 3

Security in God

When I was a little girl in elementary school, I remember coming home from school one day and telling my mom that all of my friends at school had a "boyfriend." As for me, as long as I had my daddy, I did not need one. How did I know and understand the magnitude of the security my dad provided me? I am not sure if I understood why or if I could articulate it; however I knew and understood its effects. I knew it was something that equated to having enough, and that I had no need for what I saw others seeking after.

This is the security Father God wants us to have in Him. We saw the reason that He was the first one that Eve saw and He was the one to present her to Adam. However, we can sometimes find ourselves so busy seeking what we need from a man that it's no wonder we end up with such heartbreak. No man can fill in us what our life and breath owe to Him. Fulfillment comes only in Him and by Him. He touches and replenishes us from the inside out. However, we are looking for love the wrong way when we go after it from the outside, hoping it will eventually or somehow turn into inside love. The most important part of who we are is not the physical aspect. No, it's the soul and this is what God desires to fill in our lives: to make us whole, complete and lacking no-good thing in Him.

My love began and ended with my father. He would always tell me how beautiful I was. He made everything better; if I had a bad day he would somehow always notice. Often I did not have to say anything – he just knew. I could go to him and talk to him about my problems and he would listen to me. I would sometimes sit on the steps outside their bedroom and cry softly under my breath even when he was asleep. He would wake up and say, "Tabby, what's the matter?" Once I told him what was bothering me, he would speak words to me that somehow changed my mood and direction of my thoughts. He would bandage up my wounds and send me back into my little world. I knew that he loved me and it did not matter that I had eight other siblings in the home. He was my daddy. My Mom would sometimes get upset with me because I would climb into his lap whenever I felt I needed his security and he would not refuse me. That security made a world of difference in my life.

He was the father to take me on my first date. He purchased

my first diamond ring, and my first rose. He would take me to the hairdresser and go shopping with me. He always came home bearing the most amazing gifts from his travels. He traveled a lot and I always looked forward to his return. I always felt safe when he was near.

I remember wanting to wear heels at around eleven years old. My mom said we would have to ask dad if you could wear heels. We did and he said no – not until I was twelve. I had to wait until I became a big girl. Well on my twelfth birthday he called me from Port of Spain, Trinidad, and said to me, "Baby, daddy has something for you." I could not wait to find out what it was. It was my first pair of black heels. The heels may have been an inch in height, if at all; however, I was the happiest little girl in the world. Surprisingly enough, it had nothing to do with the heels but more with the reason he gave them to me. It meant I was finally a big girl. I cherished these shoes and I wore them everywhere. They would give me the identity that I wanted before I was ready for it. However, when I was ready, my father gave to me the affirmation of why I wanted what I wanted and the gift I wanted because of why I wanted the heels. I had to trust that he was a good father and would give them to me when I was ready for them. I had to trust that he would not withhold them from me for any other reason other than the reason he gave me.

Father God wants us to have all of the things we desire.

However, understand that our maturity and level of responsibility have to be present before we can receive what we desire.

You may wonder about the purpose of these stories. It is because my relationship with my dad gave me a point of reference for my heavenly Father. I never completely understood God in the capacity of Father but He has shown me through my own earthly father how He has always been there. Even when I may not have understood His security, it was always there. This is what He desires for all of humanity: to come to a state of security in Him and with Him.

When I was a little girl, I shared a room with one of my sisters. There was this huge closet in the room, which housed all of our clothing, toys and shoes. It even had enough room for us to play inside. However, at night it was so scary in there that we would only venture in there in pairs because you could literally feel the fear inside. I learned when I became older it had been a nursery prior, so only God knows what took place in there for the spirit of fear to linger as it did. We had a bunk bed in our room; my sister slept on the top bunk and I slept on the bottom. She would cry and scream herself to sleep each night, I mean, literally to the point of torture. I later understood when I got older that she was actually seeing bad spirits at night.

For me, it was the exact opposite. There was this huge angel that stood at the foot of where she was laying and at the head of where I slept. I did not fear because I saw this angel every

Security in God

night standing there guarding me, and I knew I was safe. It was extremely tall and there was this bright light that reflected from him. There was this inexplicable sense of security. I never understood what she saw but at the same time I could not understand why she did not see my angel. He was so beautiful. There was so much security in knowing he was there. I knew she was afraid but I did not know how to help her. I would try to console her and say it was okay. But it did not make things better for her. On hindsight, maybe I should have told her about the angel that I saw.

We were both in the same room but had two different types of encounter each night. This is how life should be for us in this world. There should be so much security that though we see terrible things happening around us, we are not shaken or moved by them. This angel never said a word to me – and he never needed to – his very presence allowed me to know why he was there.

If we seek to remain separate and apart from God we cannot expect to receive His complete protection, provision or care. We must cast our cares upon Him and have total dependency upon Him for everything. We must not remove ourselves from this role. But first, some of us have to first find our position in Him; whatever it costs, we must get there. The Bible reveals that God presented Eve to Adam. This means He was directly responsible for her. He was the first one that she saw on the first day of her life.

This tells us that, even though woman was created for man,

she primarily belongs to God. We can take our security in the fact that He loves us and that He is concerned for our well-being. Before she knew the man, the Father-daughter relationship was already established. He wanted her to know that He was the reason for her essence and being. There was no one or anything on earth to compare with her.

So her first relationship was with Him, which is how and why she could function in the role she was designed to be for Adam. What she saw in God, she was to later see in Adam. He allowed her to see it in Him first in order to know Him; then He took her and gave her to her mate. If we could but secure ourselves in God before anything else, then everything else falls into the right order. We will meet the right person designed for us by God.

Ultimately, God is in control of our wellbeing. He is better equipped at fighting our relationship battles than we are. So, when we walk in absolute trust and security in Him, then we can operate in our God-given role. If the man does something that offends me, I am so secure in God that I know He will perfect that which concerns me. Even in our hurt and pain, we must trust Him. Through disappointment and mishaps we must stand fast and secure in the fact that He is sovereign and He reigns supreme. He knows the present, the past and the future and we are always safe in His arms.

Even when we are broken, we are still safe in Him. Brokenness is required for us to be made over again and become the

"Re-created Woman." We must also come to maturity knowing that some of our struggles in life are not solely because of people. They are part of the growth process because He is trying to work out of us internal traumas and pains for our total well-being and maturity.

God will allow certain things to surface in our lives so that we can be healed of them. But He must come first, above all our false securities, and be Lord over them. False security is when we misplace the security that belongs to Him on or after things or people. True security is the state of being free from danger or threat. Again, we find this only in Him. It does not mean unwanted things will not happen to us; however, we have the assurance that He is with us. If He allowed them to happen, there is a purpose and He knows the outcome. So we can go through challenging times with the confidence that our security is established in His protection and care.

The curse has been removed. Now we can shift back into the purpose intended for us by God. Now He can re-create the woman according to His original design. I do not know about you, but this assurance is enough for me and all of my female heirs after me. I can therefore make this declaration: "As for me and my household from generation to generation, we will serve the Lord and be the women God intended us to be from the beginning of our existence."

Chapter 4

Submission versus Subjection

Now that we have defined our security in Father God, we can move into His purpose for needing us to submit to His will. Submission is the action of accepting or yielding to a superior force or to the will or authority of another person. Submission is an act of faith. It has nothing to do with the quality of the character of the person to whom we are submitting. The Greek word hupotasso means a voluntary placement of yourself under the authority and leadership of another (see Ephesians 5:22).

Submission began in Genesis 1:27 when God made male and female in submission to Him and made all other life forms on earth in submission to Adam. Although the man and the woman are equal in essence and in nature, they carry about them different roles and there is a line of authority. It is vital that we go back to the original design to re-establish the right foundation. We must view everything as it was instituted and established by God because this will help in identifying the role of authority and submission.

Adam and Eve did not realize the honor they already had when they were given responsibility over nature. God honored Adam when He made the animals submit to him. Just as God named day and night, the earth, the stars, the sea and heaven with all their host, so did He bestow this honor upon Adam over the lower realm. God created the animal life but Adam named it. As God's representative in His image and likeness, Adam was given headship and authority over the earth and all it contained. God brought all of the animal life to him for him to identify and to name. It was when this assignment was complete that God moved into the next phase of His plan to create someone suitable for him. It was then that the attention was turned to providing a suitable companion for Adam to make up for what was missing.

In order to establish the foundation of family and the order of the home for all of mankind, we need to understand that the authority was given to Adam. In Genesis 2:24 we see how Adam in his naming role named Eve twice. Upon sight of her, he called her "woman," acknowledging that she was taken out of him, bone of his bone and flesh of his flesh. You will note he named her a second time after he shifted into disfavor as a result of his disobedience. Now Adam became separate and apart from God and likewise he identified the woman as a separate entity from him. The second name for her was "Eve," the mother of all living. Even though spiritual death was pronounced on all mankind, she was the one from whom the promised seed was to emanate. She is now named the "mother of all living" because, although she died a spiritual death in the garden, a Redeemer was promised to come through her and once again to restore this spiritual life lost by Adam.

It is here the struggle begins for her. Because she did not consider the authority of the man when she chose to disobey God, the irony is that now she is in subjection to him. This helps us to have an accurate understanding of the Word of God and His revealed plan for us and all of humanity. It helps us understand the proper foundation for the family, and the order of submission.

This order of submission is laid out in similar fashion for us throughout the New Testament. God still intends marriage to look exactly the way it did before the fall. He secured this in sending His Son Jesus who broke the curse and sorrow of subjection for the woman. He did away with the curse of being subjected to man when Jesus, representing man, became subject to the law, the Jews, Pilate, and the Sanhedrin counsel who crucified Him. This act of submission by Jesus to the will of the Father by the humiliation of the cross was something that Satan could not fathom because it was an act that brought such shame and disgrace. As a result, submission to man should be as to the Lord and should be taken and acted out graciously because we understand our role from God in relation to our husband. As the apostle Paul instructs in Colossians 3:18, "Wives submit to your husband as unto the Lord." Now the woman can submit to the man according to God's plan of submission from the beginning.

Peter provides more depth on this subject. He says that there is an order in submission. The man as the head of the family submits to God, the woman submits to the man and the children submit to them both in agreement. Therefore, the wife should submit to the husband just as the husband should exercise his God-given authority with understanding and honor towards her (1 Peter 3:1-7). In order to complete the role of submission, it has to be done unto the Lord. Submission should be mutual and out of respect. Authority is never to be used as a tool against another.

However, if we have not embraced the will of God for women in general, it will be difficult and even impossible to adopt a posture such as this. We must first submit ourselves to God in agreement with His will for us and not our independent wills. The option of an independent will is surrendered here to demonstrate the purity of our submission. The qualifying condition is "as unto the Lord," or else why offer the service to Him if this is not your desire? Our desires must be to submit to Him with

Submission versus Subjection

the same fervency and seriousness as we would if we were called to be used by God to accomplish a major assignment for Him.

I will borrow the words of Kathryn Kuhlman when she said she remembered the day she died. That was the day she surrendered her will to God. We must decide the day that we will choose to die to our will and our intent to govern our own lives too. I have been married three times and I cannot honestly say that I committed myself to total submission to either of my first two husbands. I always found a way to find a flaw in the system, or in their character or deeds to exempt me from being able to carry this out in obedience. This is not to say I was a bad wife. However, I was not obedient to God or submissive to their authority in certain matters.

I once asked a pastor what is meant by submitting to a man and what did it look like. He told me, it is the same reverence you would give to your boss at work. Though this was almost twenty-five years ago, I never fully grasped the principle until now. In the meantime, I had no idea of what was working against me; but now I know it was the curse of subjection – "Your desire *shall be* for your husband, and he shall rule over you" (Genesis 3:16). And so we see that Eve's disregard for the role of her husband brought sorrow to herself.

How many of us are like that? It's amazing how a woman can suffer the pangs of childbirth but fail to come to a place of godly submission to her husband. She will almost die to bear a child for him but not submit to him. Submission is not determined by whether the man's character deserves it or not. This is where it hurts. You do not submit because you can trust him either: you trust because you have submitted to God. Everything hinges on that. To do it the right way, is to do it God's way. Knowing you are safe in His care, you can be assured that when conflicts arise, He will resolve them on your behalf and for the well-being of your entire household.

Submission is easy when the will is not involved. If there is nothing in us to buck or to resist what we are to submit to, there will be no resistance in submission in that particular area. However, if the will is resistant to giving in, there will be no possible way to submit, first to God and then to man. Whenever there is resistance to the truth, we must investigate our will to discover what is hiding in the darkness, arrest the stronghold and pull it down. This will empower us to make a conscientious decision based on the truth.

How did the gentle act of submission devolve into the brutal act of subjection?

Let's go back to the Garden and examine Eve's choice.

The Dilemma of Choice

Until the moment of her dialogue with the serpent, Eve's only source of knowledge came from Adam. Suddenly she found

Submission versus Subjection

herself with the ability to access knowledge from another source. I am certain this new dimension of knowledge presented by this wise creature was intriguing to her.

In her choice to disobey, Eve gave herself over to the pursuit of self-knowledge and self-gratification based on pride. That decision was disastrous. Now, cast out of her ideal world, she finds herself subjected to Adam. No longer an equal partner with him, she is now under his domination and rule. He lost dominion over the natural realm but gained it over the woman. Having both lost his God-given identity, Adam had to learn how to survive in a strange and hostile environment outside the garden, and now he had to navigate through this new state of living while dragging the woman with him.

As a result of her decision her sentence was two-fold: a condition of sorrow and the debased position of subjection. The trauma to which she exposed herself (and hitherto all women) in her pursuit of independence, the hardship, the hurt and pain were all a result of her choice. This is a sober lesson to all of us to pay heed to our choices and, better yet, know why we are choosing to make certain decisions. The fruit of our lives is the consequence of our choice.

I mentioned earlier when I was younger and would read the Bible, it seemed as if God had given the woman to the man to be abused by him with no restitution. She is mistreated by man in her unguarded and unprotected state, just as Lot felt free to give his two daughters over to be raped by the men in the street (see Genesis 19:8). Now I understand why Eve, with her choice, was responsible for multiplying the sorrows upon all women. In suffering the consequences of her actions, she not once considered her husband or her progeny – all women. Now she is put into sorrow and subjugation. To submit now becomes a curse upon the woman; this means prior to her sin, she was equal to Adam: equal but with different roles of responsibility. Now she finds herself completely debased.

It is here we lay the ax to the root of the tree for the misuse of the woman. We can remove the blinders to have a clear view. I was told after I had my daughter that guilt comes with being a mommy. However, I have a better understanding that it is not guilt: it is sorrow. All of the sorrows of the woman are all due to the curse imputed to us by Eve's disobedience. Here is our true enemy: a state of sorrow and of subjection. We can label and categorize them all here. It is here the mind should obtain a proper perspective and start to re-categorize all of our sorrows and hardships in this life. It should then be easy to forgive and let go now.

I can see here, how some men adopt the perception that a woman, regardless of how she is treated by them and regardless of what they do, must submit to them. He does not place her in fertile soil, but expects by virtue of being male, the harvest that comes with having a wife and family. He expects this, not as the consequences of his actions or a lack thereof but because he knows the woman must submit to him. So submission is abused and this authority is not properly exercised. This is why most men do not bother to educate themselves on being godly husbands and fathers. They hold the idea, "This is what she is supposed to do because it is her role and duty to be subjected to me regardless of how I treat her. So, on my part, I can uphold myself alone, and not give myself completely to her as Christ has done for the church. I can still operate outside of this principle and demand what I expect and want because she is subjected to me."

This is why a man will vow to protect her from danger or from an outside enemy or intruder, but not from himself. In his "I will take a bullet for you and I will give you my last to secure you," he is saying, "I know I am supposed to love you and protect you. I will do this when you are in danger or if push comes to shove. I love you enough to die for you but I will not love you enough to give up my everyday life for you. I will love you in death but I will not love you to the death of myself in life."

This is also why a man will have an extramarital affair. Often it is not because he is in love with the other woman but because he is in love with himself. He sees what he chooses and how he applies his affection as loving on himself with his time, his resources and commitments. I have asked why a man would take the best of himself and give it to a woman outside of the home rather than make that investment in his wife? Yet he complains about the harvest he receives from her. There is a divinely appointed principle that what you sow, you reap. When he receives the harvest of his poor sowing, he blames the woman for causing it. It becomes her burden to bear rather than his responsibility to initiate.

The response I received to my question was, "I married you and I loved you but I did not give myself to you. I kept myself. It was a selfish thing to do, but that is what I did." So much in this moment now makes sense to me. Everything I failed to grasp in my heart and mind as to why things happened the way they did, all of the pieces suddenly came together like a puzzle.

I also have to wonder why the God-given love in the heart of Adam was not present. Did he resent Eve for enticing him to eat the fruit knowing the consequences? I believe that man has taken up this offense against the woman by this subjugation. I can imagine that in their new found state, he passed down the history of his frustration toward the woman. I believe this because he blamed her in front of God. Where there is no true respect or value for the women, here is where it comes into play. The man uses every occasion to blame her for his choices and his lack of character. I believe the resentment has been passed down through the seed of man, and to that extent it has become ingrained in his nature.

Now that we have a clear view of Eve's choice, we will move forward with the tactic and tool she used on Adam and see how this tool impacted and continues to impact the female gender.

Chapter 5

The Power of Influence

We will begin this chapter with a review of the concept of Influence and its derivatives, manipulation and persuasion. Influence is the capacity to have an effect on the character, development or behavior of someone or something. It implies the power of producing an effect without apparent exertion or force or direct exercise of command. The exercise of the power of influence is in itself good as long as it is used according to how God intended its use. However, all things apart from Him come from a corrupt state.

Manipulation takes influence a step further. Manipulation is to control or to play upon another by artful, unfair means to one's own advantage. Its purpose is to control another person in an insidious way, especially by distorting their perception of reality. Manipulation is therefore a dishonest form of influence and it is most often used at the expense of others.

Persuasion is the ability to move others to a desired action or goal by playing on their emotions. The purpose is to use a positive means of persuasion to turn a negative situation around. Take Abigail, who faced with crisis when her husband Nabal refused to supply David with provision, and persuaded David not to retaliate (1 Samuel 25). Then there was Ruth, faced with separation from Naomi, who clung to her mother-in-law and persuaded her to let her go back to Israel with her (Ruth 1:16-17). Look at Deborah who sent for Barak to gather the tribes together to fight against the Canaanites on the promise that she would lead the battle (Judges 4:4-7). Each of these women was faced with a difficult challenge. However, by taking on a proactive role, the women used their weight to change the behavior of people and thereby turned a threat into an opportunity for good.

The serpent's target was Adam all of the time. He had to bring down the head of the household. However, he knew he could only undermine him in an indirect way, so he used Eve. By his method of seducing her through her appetite, his strategy was carried out according to plan. She fell for his beguiling words and never saw what was coming. She never thought that this charming, attentive creature would use her to destroy her own house by the work of her own hand. She handed Adam the fruit, effectively allowing the enemy access to him through her. She did not care how this would impact their future; all she cared about was the here and now. So she allowed a temporary moment to cause her to make a permanent decision.

Let us step back and look at what Eve chose to do with her power of influence. This will help us to understand who we are and how we operate. Essentially, Eve was saying to her husband, "I know this is wrong but here – take it anyway. I know you will not refuse me." She did not speak out the underlying truth: "The serpent knows this too, which is why he is using me to get to you. Rather than abide by the Word of God, my appetite has whetted in me a lust to be filled with the things he promised. See now, I took it and nothing happened … why don't you too?" She never gave him a thought. This is one of the main reasons men struggle with giving their hearts over to women totally; we may be deceived but they know what is in us. How did Eve use her power of influence? She used it to sway her husband. Her strength became her weakness and that of humanity.

We can see the same traits of fallen woman and their effects reverberate throughout the Bible: how women have used this power for their own personal gain and brought about sorrow.

Sarah

We can begin with the case of Sarah, the wife of Abraham. Rather than remain in faith, believing in God for their miracle child (because she was barren and now old), Sarah decided to assist God in bringing about the promised seed. She persuaded Abraham to cohabit with her servant Hagar. However, this plan did not work out as expected. It worked to the detriment of not only herself and Abraham but also Hagar and the son Ishmael. This brought division into her home. The servant Hagar now despised her because she had brought forth a son and Sarah could not. This gave her an advantage. But it was short-lived. Eventually, once the promised child was born of Abraham and Sarah, Hagar and her son Ishmael were cast out of Abraham's home and family. The consequences were far-reaching: they formed the Arab nation who are constantly at enmity with Israel right up to this day.

Rebekah

Abraham and Sarah's son Isaac had twin sons, Esau and Jacob, from his wife Rebekah. Even during delivery God had told Rebekah there were two nations in her womb and the elder would serve the younger. When the time came for their father Isaac to bestow a special blessing on the elder son Esau, as was the custom, Rebekah pressed upon Jacob to usurp his brother's blessing by tricking the father. In her twisted way to make sure the major promise of God went to her favorite, she used deception and caused great sorrow to her family. Knowing that the elder son, Esau, had already handed over his birthright to his younger brother for a bowl of soup, she now had Jacob impersonate his brother when receiving the blessing of the father, who had failing eyesight. In one day, Rebekah destroyed her family by betraying Isaac and Esau with her treacherous plan. As a result she never saw her son Jacob again because he was forced to flee for his life to his uncle's home in a distant country. Although Jacob was blessed to find a bride, Rachel, he reaped the sowing of his mother's follies multiple times through the ill treatment of her brother Laban.

Jezebel (1 Kings chapters 17-18)

King Ahab was controlled by his evil wife Jezebel, and became one of the wickedest kings in Israel's history. A Baal worshiper steeped in the occult, she turned Ahab's heart away from God. She incited him to commit pre-meditated murder by wrongly accusing a man whose vineyard Ahab coveted. She slew the prophets of God and instituted her own false prophets of Baal. As a consequence, the northern kingdom turned towards apostasy, which brought about great hardship and famine to the nation. The prophet Elijah pronounced judgment upon this nation and it did not rain for three and half years according to his word.

Delilah (Judges 16:4-30)

Like Jezebel, Samson's wife Delilah had the power of influence and used it for evil purposes. In the story of Samson and Delilah, Samson taunted the Philistines with his great strength and won many battles against them. Nobody knew that his strength came from his long hair, which as a Nazirite, he had vowed never to cut. But the Philistine woman, Delilah, whom he loved, tricked Samson into telling her his secret. At first he made up all kinds of stories but she kept on pressuring him. How did he not see it coming? So finally he told her, "My strength is in the locks of my hair. If my hair is cut I will become like the average man." As he slept, Delilah had his hair cut and handed him over to his enemies. He was captured, blinded, and enslaved by the Philistines. The woman he loved and in whom he confided his vital secret betrayed him. She brought down the strongest man of her day.

However, her treachery was not without consequence. I am certain she was present on the day of celebration, when they all gathered to make a sport of their enemy. A man who once dominated their entire city was now sightless and had to be led to the temple of Dagon by a little lad. He requested the lad to place him between the two main pillars that supported the temple and petitioned the Lord to give him one last wave of strength. The Lord answered that plea. Singlehandedly, he pushed the two pillars, demolishing the great temple and destroying his captors and himself. So Delilah's gloating was short-lived because on that day he destroyed more Philistines than he had in all his lifetime. Delilah's choice caused the destruction of her own people. Grave consequences indeed!

By contrast, let us look at three ordinary women in the Bible who rose to the challenge with integrity, and reversed the situation for their lives and posterity.

Ruth - loyal friend (Book of Ruth)

Ruth, a Moabite, was the daughter-in-law of Naomi now dwelling in Moab. After Naomi lost her husband and her two sons in Moab, she gathered her belongings and began her journey back to Bethlehem, the house of bread. The famine in Israel was now over and she could return. She entreated her two daughters-in-law to return to their parents with hopes of finding marriage again. Orpah did just that. However, Ruth clung to her, and vowed to follow her and embrace her culture, her faith, her God, her struggle even to death.

Once they were settled in Bethlehem, Ruth went out to glean in the grain fields. The Bible says that she happened to fall on a parcel of land that belonged to Boaz, a well-respected man of the community, who happened to be a kinsman of Naomi's husband. Divine providence was at work here because Ruth had chosen the will of God for her life. In fact, Boaz had heard of her before he met her. He noticed a lovely stranger gleaning on his property and was informed that she was the Moabite woman. Boaz gave her permission to glean from his fields and pronounced a blessing on her, offering her security and protection from any male harassment. At midday he would have a meal with her and their friendship blossomed over the harvesting period.

Naomi, being a wise woman, could see the developing relationship between Ruth and Boaz and advised her on how to initiate the next move. The harvest was over and it was now the threshing season. Knowing that Boaz would be sleeping at night at the threshing floor, Ruth was to present herself to him when he was sleeping, dressed in her best garments. When Boaz discovered Ruth lying beside him, he was shocked. But Ruth, using the carefully rehearsed words given by her mother-in-law, entreated Boaz to "spread therefore thy covering over me for thou art a near kinsman." This was in effect a proposition of marriage.

Boaz commended her for her virtuous character. Although he was a much older man, he was pleased that she did not choose a young man closer to her age. It was her character that left such an impression on him. Please get this: it was her character and not her body that gave him such high regard for her. He assured her he would not rest until he had finalized all the procedures for taking her as his wife. He could have chosen to dishonor her in secret but he honored her because she carried herself as a woman of faith in her God.

So the marriage was blessed by the community, and in due course Ruth and Boaz had a son, Obed, and Naomi had a grandson who gave her a new outlook in life. Now note this: Obed was the father of Jesse, the father of David and David was the forefather of Jesus the Messiah. So, surprisingly, Ruth a Moab, was honored to be in the lineage of the Messiah. All because she followed the leading of God for her destiny.

Not only Ruth but also Rahab the mother of Boaz was a foreigner, a Canaanite. Who was this Rahab? She was rescued from the conquest of Jericho and had married a Jew, Salmon. So there was a gentle spot here that God had woven into the lineage of David. Two unlikely women found themselves in the will of God and not just in the lineage of David, but for the good of all humanity. We will discuss Rahab in more detail in chapter 9.

Esther – rising to the call (Book of Esther)

God was able to use Esther by bringing her to center stage to save the children of Israel. In the days of the Persian empire, Queen Vashti had so displeased the Persian king when she refused to attend a banquet that she was removed from her royal position. The search began for a new queen, and Mordecai presented to the palace his cousin, Hadassah, who adopted her other name Esther to conceal her Jewish identity. Esther so pleased the king that in due course, he made her his queen.

Mordecai was hated by one of the king's high-ranking officers, Haman, because this Jewish man did not bow to him. Out of spite, Haman turned the king against the Jews and persuaded him to issue a proclamation that would result in the annihilation of the Jewish population residing in the kingdom.

Esther could have enjoyed safety within the walls of the palace and it was a major struggle for her to do as Mordecai requested: influence the king on behalf of her people. This itself was fraught with danger, for anyone who approached the king without invitation could lose their life. Finally, realizing that she was raised "for such a time as this," Esther called for a three-day fast among her people throughout the land. She too fasted and waited as a weapon in the hand of God for her people and, when it was time to move, she moved. Her words, "If I perish let me perish" showed her resolve. What in fact she was saying was, "I am going before the king. I am going against the law and decree of this nation to put forward my case and putting my life on the line for my people. However, I choose to do it because I know Almighty God is with me." Then, summoning up all her courage she enters the courtroom of the king's palace resplendent in her royal robes.

Because she allowed the will of God to operate through her, this young woman found favor in the king's sight, not once but twice. The king's favor was demonstrated when he allowed her to enter the palace and accepted her invitation to a two-day banquet which included the enemy Haman. On the second day of the banquet, Haman's evil plot against the Jews was exposed. Once again, the king's favor was upon Esther as he chose to believe her and not the evil Haman. That day Haman was hanged on the very gallows he had built for Mordecai.

Esther became the most powerful woman in the entire kingdom as she and Mordecai wrote the decree to allow all of the Jews in every providence to defend themselves against the previous decree that had been launched against them. God was able to use Esther to overturn the schemes of Haman, which ultimately showed satanic influence against God's people. God used one woman to save an entire nation because she was not afraid to go against a royal decree to save them.

Abigail – averting a crisis (I Samuel 25:1-42)

Like Esther, Abigail used her influence in the household for the protection of her family and all within their sphere of influence – staff, cattlemen, and farm workers. Knowing the ignorance and gross behavior of her husband, she moved hastily to meet the request of David for supplies. She used her wisdom, her grace, her powerful persuasion and her positive words to defuse his anger toward Nabal. As a result David did not retaliate.

The ReCreated Woman

In this account we see how God used this woman to single-handedly take down a four-hundred-man army with no physical weapons. Clothed only with wisdom, she was able to disarm David from within. She was no match for him in war but she appealed to his character. She disarmed him with her words. She persuaded him to do good and not evil, even though he had every right to do so. She talked him down from the height of rage and reminded him of the consequences of his choice for the future. Her appeal to him was to let her have an audience with him before he let his fury run loose.

She acknowledged the wrongdoing of her husband in insulting David's men with his pride and arrogance. She also spoke a word of prophecy into his life. The Lord will fight this battle for him, not just this one but the one he was facing with King Saul (verse 30). She kept him from carrying offense in his heart and from shedding blood causelessly by taking matters into his own hands. She had confidence in God and she assured him that He would deal with her husband. All she requested of David was that "when the LORD shall have dealt well with my lord, then remember thine handmaid" (verse 31).

And David responded, "Blessed be the LORD God of Israel, which sent thee this day to meet me: And blessed be thy advice, and blessed be thou, which hast kept me this day from coming to shed blood, and from avenging myself with mine own hand" (verses 32-33).

The Power of Influence

Although in the end Nabal died of natural causes, it was not by the hand of King David. David remembered his promise to Abigail and took her with him to be his wife.

These are the true characteristics of a three-dimensional woman, where beauty of body, soul and spirit converge.

It is true that God fashioned the woman for the man. However, we must also understand man was in a perfect state when God presented the woman to him. Some men use the scripture to say that God was obliged to make woman subservient to man. They argue that Adam was made before her, installed in his God-given office and operated from a position of authority. But we are now flawed beings operating in an imperfect world. As it stands, men do not know how to handle the prized possession that God handed them. It is not until they have gone through the renewal process and reposition themselves properly in God that they will understand their role and be equipped to operate in it fully.

Man's true appreciation and value for woman comes only after he has allowed himself to be completely made over by God. He will then understand why God made her for him and what she is to be to him. Without such an understanding, she will continue to be damaged and broken. This is the reason the word says to husbands to love their wives and not be bitter towards them.

As women, let us take a moment to consider how we have

chosen to exercise all of the gifts and talents God has given to us. Let us reflect on our misuse of them and how different the outcomes could have been. With hindsight, what did this misuse do to us? How could we have better defined our choices and made better use of our intentions and motives? How would it have impacted our sphere of influence in our culture, our marriages, families, careers, and the raising of our children?

In the next chapter let's consider the most extreme form of manipulation: seduction.

Chapter 6

The Spirit of Seduction

As we begin this discussion on seduction, we will start by defining this devious character trait. Seduction is to persuade to disobedience or disloyalty, or to lead astray, usually by persuasion or false promises. How did it originate? If we go back to the beginning in Genesis 3 we can see a vivid display of it in operation. Here the serpent uses seduction to stimulate the senses and emotions to persuade Eve. He appealed to four of her senses: sight, touch, taste and smell that triggered her emotions.

But to unveil how and where the first act of seduction came into being, we must look further back – into eternity past. Here we see the appearance of Lucifer, whose name means "bearer of light" or "morning star." Lucifer was once a high-level angel who served in the throne room of God but because of his activity his name devolved into "Satan," which means "accuser of the brethren."

Scripture reveals that Satan was once an anointed cherub who guarded and led in worship in the holy mountain of God

Ezekiel 28:13-17 NKJV:

> "You *were* the anointed cherub who covers;
>
> I established you;
>
> You were on the holy mountain of God ... (verse 14)
>
> "The workmanship of your timbrels and pipes
>
> Was prepared for you on the day you were created" (verse 13)

Not only did he have a high calling, he was perfect in beauty and wisdom:

> "You *were* the seal of perfection,
>
> Full of wisdom and perfect in beauty ..." (verse 12)

However, because of his beauty, wisdom and excessive trading, he became prideful and corrupt:

> "Your heart was lifted up because of your beauty;

You corrupted your wisdom for the sake of your splendor ..." (verse 17)

"By the abundance of your trading

You became filled with violence within,

And you sinned ..." (verse 16)

Isaiah 14 tells us how pride and ambition seduced him into believing that he could exalt himself above the position of God. Thus he pronounced his five famous "I wills":

Isaiah 14:12-16 NKJV:

"For you have said in your heart:

'**I will** ascend into heaven,

I will exalt my throne above the stars of God;

I will also sit on the mount of the congregation

On the farthest sides of the north;

I will ascend above the heights of the clouds,

I will be like the Most High.'

Yet you shall be brought down to Sheol,

To the lowest depths of the Pit .

"Those who see you will gaze at you,

And consider you, *saying:*

> '*Is* this the man who made the earth tremble,
>
> Who shook kingdoms …'"

Lucifer's mind was captivated by the false premise that he was on the same level as God and could set up his throne higher than God himself. What deception coming from a created being like us! It's the worst kind of deception for someone to allow his own intellect and knowledge to become so distorted that they give rise to vain imaginations and ambitions.

This perverted notion of his own brightness caused him to oppose the will and plan of God for his life. He revolted against the God Most High and persuaded a third of the angelic host of heaven to follow him (Revelation 12:7-9). They were cast down into "the heavenlies," where they continue to conduct warfare to obstruct the purposes of God and to influence humankind (Daniel 10:13).

We should not be surprised that Satan reared his head in the Garden. Who was his target? Knowing that man is God's most prized creation, made in the image and likeness of Him, he aimed his fury at us. Very likely his heart was filled with resentment that this latest creation could be exalted above him in stature. Psalm 8:4 is full of wonder at this: "What is man, that thou art mindful of him? and the son of man, that thou visitest him?" This could very well be Satan's envious cry, "What is man that he should be made to be higher than me?"

Having been a worship leader in heaven, he now coveted both man's allegiance and worship. The creature he chose to use in his scheme against mankind was the serpent, who was known for its cunning, "Now the serpent was more cunning than any beast of the field which the LORD God had made" (Genesis 3:1 NKJV).

What strategy did the serpent use? He approached Eve. He knew that Adam had received direct revelation from God and had a solid understanding of the command. On the other hand, Eve only heard from Adam and was placed below him in the line of authority. What method was he going to use? Intimidation? Fear tactics? No, a soft and sly approach: seduction.

The first step in the process was to befriend her and cause her to believe him and trust him. So he approached her in a casual way and presented himself as a caring ally of hers who possessed much wisdom. His next step was to undermine her confidence in her Creator. Again, he would not do this by a frontal attack. No, he would do this by innuendo, that is, causing her to call into question what God had said, "Has God indeed said …?" Thus doubt was planted. Having caused doubt, he took this a step further by leading her to mistrust God's good intentions and integrity. "You will not surely die. For God knows …" Then he offered the bait: "For God knows that in the day you eat of it your eyes will be opened, and **you will be like God, knowing good and evil**" (Genesis 3:4-5 NKJV).

This created desire and the woman took the bait. She saw

"the tree *was* **good** for food, that it *was* **pleasant** to the eyes, and a tree desirable to **make *one* wise** ..." (verse 6) Please catch that: this is how he has been robbing us of our continued faith to this day. What is his intent? To cause us to doubt God's word and integrity, to persuade us of his own care and concern for us, to entice us by drawing us in out of curiosity, and to assail our mind with hidden information apart from God that would arouse new desires and expectations.

We saw how Lucifer as one of the most beautiful angels created by God is the master of seduction and deception and how he planted within Eve the seed of seduction. He knew her vulnerability: her subordinate role of authority in the family unit. What was her potential weapon? Her beauty and power of influence over her husband. He could use both of these to his advantage if she could tempt him.

Similarly, Satan comes as our friend but he has no ability to do any good. He is only capable of evil. Just the way he appeared to Eve as a benevolent creature, he can appear to us as an "angel of light" to perfect his disguise. And as he plants his seed of seduction within us, we see those very traits appearing as second nature to us. This is the signal that the enemy is at work within us to control and seduce others.

With this in mind, it is easier to understand the words of Solomon revealed in the Book of Proverbs concerning the strange Woman.

The Strange Woman

The wisest king that ever lived had 700 wives and 300 concubines. Needless to say, he had a lot of experience with women – and I can imagine a lot to say about them! Solomon refers to the immoral woman, who chooses to live without any standards, as the "strange woman."

Here you can see the same principles of seduction at play in greater detail. The strange woman poses as your friend in helping you find your greatest satisfaction in her, in safety, comfort and privacy. Note well the way she approaches you with her flattery and enticements: the words that fall from her lips drop as honey from the honeycomb and her mouth is smoother than oil (Proverbs 5:3).

What is her background? She could be a prostitute but not necessarily so – just a promiscuous woman who has forsaken all standards of morality and forgotten her covenant with her God. She is careless and gives no thought to her way of life or her aimless path.

Who are her victims? She derives pleasure from preying on the young and simple-minded, tempting them to enter her house (her domain). Solomon warns his sons to flee from her presence and to avoid her at all costs, for her house is the dwelling place of death. Proverbs 9 tells us that this woman makes boisterous demands and lacks wisdom. She lures the simple-minded who walk straightaway on to her path. She whets their appetite with the element of adventure telling them how stolen water is sweet and bread eaten in secret is pleasant. And so her victim goes in not aware that her guests are seated in the very depths of hell (Proverbs 9:13-18; see also Proverbs 2:16-20; Proverbs 5:3-6; Proverbs 6:24-26; Proverbs 7:5-23).

Proverbs 7 brings all the warnings together in describing in slow motion the process of being snared. The woman doesn't have to come for this foolish young man because he is lured to wander into her domain out of his own curiosity and lustful promptings. Notice it is in the dark of night where no one can see him. Here he will find her in her provocative attire ready and waiting.

Proverbs 7:7-23:

> I perceived among the youths,
>
> A young man devoid of understanding,
>
> Passing along the street near her corner;
>
> And he took the path to her house
>
> In the twilight, in the evening,
>
> In the black and dark night.
>
> And there a woman met him,
>
> With the attire of a harlot, and a crafty heart.
>
> She was loud and rebellious,

The Spirit of Seduction

> Her feet would not stay at home.
>
> At times she was outside, at times in the open square,
>
> Lurking at every corner.

She now takes the offensive:

> So she caught him and kissed him;
>
> With an impudent face she said to him:
>
> "I have peace offerings with me;
>
> Today I have paid my vows.
>
> So I came out to meet you,
>
> Diligently to seek your face,
>
> And I have found you."

Notice how she throws rituals into it to make things appear right. Then she further entices him with the imagery of her words which create exotic color, sensations, and aromas.

> "I have spread my bed with tapestry,
>
> Colored coverings of Egyptian linen.
>
> I have perfumed my bed
>
> With myrrh, aloes, and cinnamon."

And finally she presents the opportunity for unrestrained pleasure:

> "Come, let us take our fill of love until morning;
>
> Let us delight ourselves with love.
>
> For my husband is not at home;
>
> He has gone on a long journey;
>
> He has taken a bag of money with him,
>
> And will come home on the appointed day."

Sadly, this is the fate of the ignorant young lover:

> With her enticing speech she caused him to yield,
>
> With her flattering lips she seduced him.
>
> Immediately he went after her, as an ox goes to the slaughter,
>
> Or as a fool to the correction of the stocks,
>
> Till an arrow struck his liver.
>
> As a bird hastens to the snare,
>
> He did not know it would cost his life.

Solomon warns his sons to stay away from the profoundly immoral woman, who flatters with her tongue. Protect yourself from being lured to her bosom, he says. She is a stranger, so do not desire her embrace (Proverbs 6:24-26). Do not lust for her beauty in your heart, for by her men are brought to poverty. Whoever commits adultery with such a woman lacks understanding and destroys his own soul. Wounds and dishonor will come to him and his shame will never be wiped away (Proverbs 6:32-33). For she has cast down many wounded, and all who were slain by her were strong *men*. Her house *is* the way to hell, descending to the chambers of death (Proverbs 7:26-27).

In contrast to the woman who attracts through seduction, Solomon also paints a picture of the woman who repels because of her disagreeable nature. We will meet her in the next chapter. Solomon certainly had a lot of experience with women!

Chapter 7

The Contentious Woman

It is better to live in a corner of the housetop [on the flat roof, exposed to the weather] than in a house shared with a quarrelsome (contentious) woman (Proverbs 25:24 AMP).

Solomon is speaking here of the woman who refuses to submit to her husband and to respect his God-given authority over her. These are the characteristics of a quarrelsome or a contentious woman. Do you recognize some of them around you?

These are further scriptures in Proverbs that describe her:

> Better to live in a corner of the roof than share a house with a quarrelsome wife (Proverbs 21:9 NIV).
>
> Better to live in a desert than with a quarrelsome and nagging wife (Proverbs 21:19 NIV).
>
> A quarrelsome wife is as annoying as constant dripping on a rainy day. Stopping her complaints is like trying to stop the wind or trying to hold something with greased hands (Proverbs 27:15 NLT).

Quarrelsomeness is a characteristic of the woman who is inclined to argue, is fond of disputing and enjoys controversy. She is quick to respond and slow to listen. She rarely asks questions to gain understanding, because her intent is to accuse or to continue to press her case. This woman is combative and always ready for an argument. She is continuously at loggerheads with people or engaged in hostility. She thrives on personal combat. She even has an ill-natured readiness to fight without a cause. She harbors a perverse fondness for initiating arguments and disputes, and is ready to quarrel even in petty matters.

A quarrelsome wife devalues her husband, and disrespects and undermines his authority by her words and actions. She persistently finds fault with him and has the habit of nagging. No wonder he retreats to the corner of the roof! It is an embarrassing thing to know this is written about us in the Bible to the degree that God saw fit to allow Solomon to put this kind of character on display.

I am certain this was probably heightened by the fact Solomon did have encounters with the thousand or so women living in his household, seven hundred of them being his wives. Can you imagine the bickering among them for his time, attention and favors? Sadly, Solomon's words remain true even in our day.

Where did this contentious spirit originate? I believe the source is once again the Garden. When God asked Adam whether he had eaten the fruit, he pointed to "the woman" – not my wife, bones of my bones, flesh of my flesh – no, "the woman." She was to blame. When asked about her part in it, Eve put the blame on the serpent.

> Hast thou eaten of the tree, whereof I commanded thee that thou shouldest not eat?
>
> And the man said, **The woman whom thou gavest** to be with me, she gave me of the tree, and I did eat.
>
> And the LORD God said unto the woman, What is this that thou hast done? And the woman said,

> The serpent beguiled me, and I did eat (Genesis 3:11-13, emphasis added).

Already there was division between the two that once saw themselves as one flesh. I believe that the spirit of contention or strife was sown in that moment. It emerged soon after when their son Cain was envious of his brother Abel and went out and murdered him. And it continues to this day as people resort to disputes to solve problems and nation strives with nation for territory and power.

The spirit of strife stands out among the works of the flesh named by Paul in Galatians 5.

> Now the works of the flesh are evident, which are: adultery, fornication, uncleanness, lewdness, idolatry, sorcery, **hatred, contentions, jealousies, outbursts of wrath, selfish ambitions, dissensions, heresies, envy, murders,** drunkenness, revelries, and the like; of which I tell you beforehand, just as I also told *you* in time past, that those who practice such things will not inherit the kingdom of God (Galatians 5:19-21 NKJV, emphasis added).

They operate from the carnal mind which is controlled by the flesh and all its appetites. Unlike the fruit of the Holy Spirit which embraces peace, gentleness and self-control, these works are apparent in the person who is not submitted to the will of God. Neither do they submit to the line of authority God has designated in the home, the workplace or even the church.

Strife in the Church

Well aware of the strife that can take place in the church, Paul also gives instructions for the conduct of older and younger women to ensure an atmosphere of peace and harmony.

Older women – role models

Older women are to be examples to the younger women of moral values and godly conduct in the home:

> Likewise, teach the older women to be reverent in the way they live, not to be slanderers or addicted to much wine, but to teach what is good. Then they can urge the younger women to love their husbands and children, to be self-controlled and pure, to be busy at home, to be kind, and to be subject to their husbands, so that no one will malign the word of God (Titus 2:3-5 NIV).

Younger widows – practice restraint

Some of the younger women in Timothy's day mirror the women in Proverbs 2:16-19 and Proverbs 7:5-23. As they became wanton in their ways, they cast off their first faith, and become idle with their time and hands. They wander from house to house as tattlers and busy bodies using their mouths to speak loosely. To avoid this kind of behavior it was recommended that the women marry, bear children, and guide the household. They should give no occasion to the enemy by speaking anything of reproach but rather make an earnest effort to become a godly woman (see 1 Timothy 5:13-15).

Submission

We are to be an example of Christ's church in submission and obedience to Him and those to whom He delegates authority in all things (Ephesians 5:22-24). Paul admonishes us to submit to our own husbands. The tone is almost one of rebuke because many of us will submit to our bosses, our pastors, or whatever great prophet or apostle who comes into town – all other men but not our own. Submission is our duty and it is pleasing to the Lord when we submit to the husband as if something done directly unto the Lord Himself (Colossians 3:18).

To the married woman, Paul says: "Wives, submit to your own husbands, as to the Lord" (Ephesians 5:22 NKJV). Peter agrees, "Wives, likewise, *be* submissive to your own husband." A wise woman can use her quiet chaste behavior to win over her husband even if he does not walk in obedience to the word. We must therefore exemplify godly character in all that we do. Our focus must not be on the outward adorning but the adorning of the inner self with godly character (1 Peter 3:1-6). Our aim should not be to undermine our husbands or attempt to usurp their authority (I Timothy 2:12).

Likewise, Paul says,

> I desire therefore that … the women adorn themselves in modest apparel, with propriety and moderation, not with braided hair or gold or pearls or costly clothing, but, which is proper for women professing godliness, with good works (1 Timothy 2:8, 9-10 NKJV).

Here we can see the clear admonition to women not to call attention to themselves by their showy apparel but let their hidden beauty come through in their quiet unassuming behavior.

Silence in the church

For this reason Paul instructed the women of the church at Corinth to keep silent and not be permitted to speak in church. He understood the reproach that those women had brought upon the church and their husbands, and his intention was to curb this unruly behavior. The following admonition of Paul's has been widely debated as to whether it should be interpreted as a general guideline concerning all women or specific women in a particular context.

> Let your women keep silent in the churches, for they are not permitted to speak; but *they are* to be submissive, as the law also says. And if they want to learn something, let them ask their own husbands at home; for it is shameful for women to speak in church (1 Corinthians 14:33-35 NLT).

Paul gives the same advice to his young pastor Timothy:

> Let a woman learn in silence with all submission. And I do not permit a woman to teach or to have authority over a man, but to be in silence (1 Timothy 2:11-12 NKJV).

Some churches use this scripture to rule that no woman should teach the word or prophesy publicly during the church service, although they may minister to a small group. Others interpret this scripture to be addressing the disorderly conduct of some of the women in the church such as speaking out of turn during the service. If we look at the whole context of 1 Corinthians 14, we see that Paul is encouraging the free operation of the gifts of the Holy Spirit, especially the vocal gifts of prophecy and the interpretation of tongues. The exercising of these gifts should naturally include women. In the same passage Paul is also emphasizing the need for proper decorum in exercising the gifts. His priority is to maintain order. So this prohibition most likely is aimed at women who are loud and disruptive in church and these are the ones who should remain silent and discuss their views privately at home.

The power of silence

Though the Women's Right Movement encourages us to be vocal, especially in public matters, there is a time for silence and a time for speech. We must also learn the power of silence. It is a precious quality to learn how to be quiet and reserved both in word and deed, heart and mind especially when everybody else is shouting. This characteristic is developed in union with the fruit of the spirit, especially the fruit of self-control, of a quiet, meek and gentle spirit (Galatians 5:22-23). We should be quick to hear in all matters and slow to speak, giving our hearts the time to make a proper judgment in all affairs.

One of the seven desires of the heart is to be heard, and another one is to be understood. "Even fools are thought wise when they keep silent; with their mouths shut, they seem intelligent" (Proverbs 7:28 NLT). Let us also learn to keep our tongue from evil and our lips from telling lies (Psalm 34:13).

The proper use of our tongue is to speak life, to build, to encourage, to edify, and to offer heartfelt prayers and worship unto the Lord. We must learn to use it for good and not for evil, not permitting the enemy to fill our mouths with his words against ourselves and against others. We should also speak out those things that are not as though they were, calling into existence the things we want to see. Jesus said we will give an account for every idle word spoken. So let us reserve our words to act as words of life, words of power, words of praise to accomplish the purposes of God and not be driven by our feelings or emotions. These can be governed by self-control.

We've just looked at two negative aspects of woman: seduction and contention. Now it's time to look at the virtuous woman.

Chapter 8

The Virtuous Woman

An excellent wife is the crown of her husband, But she who causes shame is like rottenness in his bones (Proverbs 12:4 NKJV).

A wise woman builds her home, but a foolish woman tears it down with her own hands (Proverbs 14:10 NLT).

A beautiful woman who lacks discretion is like a gold ring in a pig's snout (Proverbs 11:22 NKJV).

Who can find a woman in our times to match the virtuous woman of Proverbs 31? The common meaning of "virtuous" implies "moral excellence in character." But the biblical interpretation is much more than that. Matthew Henry's commentary tells us: "A *virtuous woman* is a woman of spirit, who has the command of her own spirit and knows how to manage other people's, one that is pious and industrious, and a help meet for a man. *A virtuous woman* is a woman of resolution, who, having espoused good principles, is firm and steady to them, and will not be frightened with winds and clouds from any part of her duty."

This virtuous woman is a rare commodity. She has more value than the most precious of jewels. These are the characteristics of the virtuous woman that Proverbs 31 describes.

Capable and dependable

The virtuous woman is capable and can be trusted to manage the household. She is conscientious in her daily work, rising early to attend to the family's needs. Her children are well fed and clothed, and her servants are well provided for. She purchases from outside what is needed to provide nourishment to her family. She works cheerfully for her family as a reflection of her love and care for them.

She is intuitive and makes her house a home. Not only does she take care of the children and all that is required for their well-being, she is a blessing to her husband. He can trust her with the finances. His finances will not come to ruin because of her negligence or squandering of resources. Her heart has good intentions toward him, always seeking his best interests, and he in turn gives her his wholehearted trust. Because of her influence, he is a success. As an honorable man, he is highly esteemed in the community.

Resourceful and enterprising

As a student of economics, she has financial astuteness and knows how to stretch out a dollar. She knows how to bargain and how to budget wisely. She perceives her merchandise is good. She avoids those "Why did I buy this?" comments. What she does not have, she will create or produce. She is resourceful, and knows how to bring in extra income.

She is also enterprising and invests in profitable ventures that have the potential to multiply and bring forth a continuous harvest. Since she makes provision for the future, she is not afraid of a rainy day.

Fear of the Lord

What is the secret of her success? While the Proverbs 31 woman can be commended for all the wonderful things she does, the most crucial thing for her is her relationship with the Lord. She lives her entire life out of a desire to honor and serve Him. This is what makes her an exceptional woman.

It starts with the fear of the Lord. He is her rock and

foundation. She rises early to give Him her praise and to cover her household in prayer. She meets with Him before she meets with her family and receives His strength. With this strength she is able to guide her household for God. They are safe because they are all covered in scarlet: that means they are protected by the blood of Jesus. She herself is clothed in linen and purple. The linen represents strength and honor because of the righteousness of Christ and the purple is the color of royalty, for she is indeed the King's daughter (Psalm 45:14-15).

She is careful to guard her tongue and only speaks words of wisdom and kindness. There is a presence about this kind of woman. She gives care to herself and to her total being and beautifies herself because she is the bride of Christ (Revelation 22:17).

Of all the women who have done well, she surpasses them all. Her children blossom and thrive, so they continually praise and bless her. Her husband praises her, recognizing her kindness and the compassion she shows to those in need. Favor, success and beauty are available to all but only the woman who fears the Lord will be praised for her works and her noble character. God will bless her hands and cause all she does to prosper. All that is given unto her will be multiplied exponentially as well as the seed for sowing. Every wise woman builds her house but the foolish plucks it down. "He who finds a wife finds a good thing, and obtains favor from the Lord" (Proverbs 18:32 NKJV).

To my sister who is single, what does this passage say to you?

Your ministry is unto the Lord. You are hidden until you are found. You are sanctified and set apart for the glory and honor of God. You do not give your chastity away but offer it up to the Lord, and remain pure before Him untill the right time. You dress, not for the sake of the attention of men, but to be approved of by God. All your pursuits are after Him and His pleasure. He hides you in the secret place of His pavilion that He may make you complete in Him.

Adorned with Humility

What was God's intent in giving the woman beauty? He made us a crown unto our husbands, visible to appreciate. A man will admire a woman with godly characteristics and beauty more than one who appeals only to his sense of sight. All of what the world offers in its definition of beauty is designed to appeal to the sensual appetite to satisfy lust and not love. We must understand what we are signing up for when we utilize its tools, which are the mechanics of beauty. We may use flattery with our lips to get what we want. We know exactly how to use manipulation. We array ourselves with manmade beauty. We dress up and adorn ourselves to become the world's woman.

But we must pay close attention to the fine print and the terms of use of the product before exercising the use of it. We must not use its methods expecting a different outcome. When we array ourselves for attention, it is attention we will get, but, unfortunately, not the kind we desire. If the intent is to appeal to a man's appetite, he will expect you to fulfill it. How you present yourself is how he will see you, treat you and finally categorize you. That will become his expectation of you. A true man has respect for a woman who has values and standards. She is a gracious woman who attains the honor she deserves (Proverbs 11:16).

Chapter 9

God's Revelations to Women

*J*esus the Messiah liberated woman from her distorted perspectives and caused the rebirthing of a new kind of woman. Through His omniscience, God looked throughout all of the generations of mankind with a plan to redeem all in each of their generations. Each generation has grown more wicked and perverse, and there may be more creative ways to sin; but there is nothing new under the sun. And yet God is saying, "I looked through the telescope of time. I saw this generation too and I made a commitment from the beginning to redeem them. They are Mine. I love them just as I loved the first generation and each one in between."

God has provided a book with answers to all of life's questions to serve as a guide and compass. The truth is hidden in His word. We must break the seals to discover who we are. Our identity is not referenced to a social security card or a birth certificate but it is who we are as a whole entity. Let us go to the word of God and allow the Word Himself to show how He brought to women in both the Old and New Testament some of the greatest revelations of who He is.

Mary Mother of Jesus

God's promise of "a seed" to Eve after the fall was not just for Eve's progeny but for all of humankind. A young virgin, Mary, found herself pregnant and the man she was betrothed to, Joseph, was contemplating divorcing her for this reproach (Matthew 18-19). But the angel Gabriel had appeared to her, and told her she would conceive and bring forth a son, the Son of God, the Christ. How would this happen? By the Holy Ghost "overshadowing" her – a miraculous conception.

The angel said to her,

> "Do not be afraid, Mary, for you have found favor with God. And behold, you will conceive in your womb and bring forth a Son, and shall call His name JESUS. He will be great, and will be called the Son of the Highest; and the Lord God

will give Him the throne of His father David. And He will reign over the house of Jacob forever, and of His kingdom there will be no end."

Then Mary said to the angel, "How can this be, since I do not know a man?"

And the angel answered and said to her, *"The Holy Spirit will come upon you, and the power of the Highest will overshadow you; therefore, also, that Holy One who is to be born will be called the Son of God"* (Luke 1:30-35 NKJV).

The angel then revealed to her that the forerunner for Christ, John the Baptist, was already in the womb of his mother, Elizabeth, Mary's cousin. Since Elizabeth had been barren, this was another miracle, for "with God all things are possible" (Luke 1:37). Mary received that astounding news with the posture of humility and the eyes of faith: "Behold the maidservant of the Lord! Let it be to me according to your word," she said (Luke 1:38).

Jesus was born flesh and bone, yet in a sinless body, a perfect body. He who knew no sin was made sin and a curse so that we might become righteous in Him (1 Corinthians 5:21). God revealed to two women who He would be and how and why He would come: through the womb of a woman conceiving by the power of the Holy Spirit and not through the seed of Adam. He began in the garden with the first woman, Eve, not just because of her but also for her. His heart is as tender to the woman as it is to man, as gentle toward her since the day He fashioned her for Adam. He loves her no less than He did when He took the time to form her.

In the following pages we will see more of His revelations that came to the least likely of women.

Rahab the Harlot

In the eyes of society, Rahab was a woman of no consequence, a common harlot operating in a inn on the wall of Jericho, one of the despised in society. But what we reject, God will use for His glory, "But God has chosen the foolish things of the world to put to shame the wise, and **God has chosen the weak things of the world to put to shame the things which are mighty**; and the base things of the world and the things which are despised …" (1 Corinthians 1:27-28 NKJV).

God used Rehab to hide two of the spies sent by Joshua to search out the city before his army moved in. God first prepared her heart by revealing to her who He was and giving her the confidence to provide the spies with the essential information they needed to enter the city.

Through all the rumors of war swirling around in the inn,

Rahab fixed her heart upon the living God and put her trust in Him alone. In her secret heart she had a sense of His power and she bound herself to Him just as Ruth would do in the generation to come. Rahab abandoned the god of her youth for the God of heaven and earth – the only true God as she defined Him. She did something with this new found faith in Him: she hid the spies and her faith was accounted to her for righteousness. God used this woman to reveal to Joshua the nature of her people. This was the report the spies would bring back to the camp; more than the physical features of the land, it was the mental state of the inhabitants towards the God of Israel.

These were Rahab's words, speaking for herself and her countrymen:

> "I know that the LORD has given you this land and that a great fear of you has fallen on us, so that all who live in this country are melting in fear because of you. We have heard how the LORD dried up the water of the Red Sea for you when you came out of Egypt, and what you did to Sihon and Og, the two kings of the Amorites east of the Jordan, whom you completely destroyed. When we heard of it, **our hearts melted** in fear and everyone's courage failed because of you, **for the LORD your God is God in heaven above and**

The ReCreated Woman

on the earth below" (Joshua 2:9-11 NIV, emphasis added).

This report would raise the morale of Joshua's armies as they entered an impregnable city fortified by its massive wall. Now the tables were turned. Forty years ago the spies returned with the report that the people of the land were giants and the Israelites were but grasshoppers in their sight (Numbers 13). Now the grasshoppers were the other side.

Rahab knew the Israelites had been triumphant in battle after battle because of Him. She allowed such great faith to arise in Him that she could make such a life-changing decision to collaborate with them to save herself and her family. She risked death for treason for betraying her nation but her loyalty had turned to the God of Abraham, Isaac and Jacob. To repay her kindness to them, Joshua granted safe passage to her and her family when Jericho was taken. Rahab was accepted by the people, married Salmon, (purportedly one of the two spies), and bore a son. She became the mother of Boaz, who as we know, married Ruth, the Moabite, and thus the lineage continued to Jesus, Son of God:

This is all explicitly stated in the first chapter of Matthew. Do you recognize some of the women we met in earlier chapters?

> [5] **Salmon begot Boaz by Rahab, Boaz begot Obed by Ruth, Obed begot Jesse, [6] and Jesse begot David the king. David the king begot**

Solomon by her *who had been the wife* of Uriah. ⁷ Solomon begot Rehoboam, Rehoboam begot Abijah, and Abijah begot Asa. ⁸ Asa begot Jehoshaphat, Jehoshaphat begot Joram, and Joram begot Uzziah. ⁹ Uzziah begot Jotham, Jotham begot Ahaz, and Ahaz begot Hezekiah. ¹⁰ Hezekiah begot Manasseh, Manasseh begot Amon, and Amon begot Josiah. ¹¹ Josiah begot Jeconiah and his brothers about the time they were carried away to Babylon.

¹² And after they were brought to Babylon, Jeconiah begot Shealtiel, and Shealtiel begot Zerubbabel. ¹³ Zerubbabel begot Abiud, Abiud begot Eliakim, and Eliakim begot Azor. ¹⁴ Azor begot Zadok, Zadok begot Achim, and Achim begot Eliud. ¹⁵ Eliud begot Eleazar, Eleazar begot Matthan, and Matthan begot Jacob. ¹⁶ **And Jacob begot Joseph the husband of Mary, of whom was born Jesus who is called Christ** (Matthew 5:5-16 NKJV, emphasis added).

So Rahab became the door and exit to and from the city, providing a place of refuge for God's people. All of the people in her country knew of the One God and the children of Israel and they all knew of their impending doom because of this

The ReCreated Woman

God of heaven and earth. But, unlike those that still clung on to their culture and their gods, she ran with the revelation she had. She abandoned her god, her people and her culture and in turn found the door of life through the spies. She was a door for them and they became a door unto her; she received them and God received her. What a beautiful portrait of the love and compassion of our God! Here was a foreign woman of great faith who acted on the word, and God had a place for her in His master plan. In Hebrews 11, you can see the name of Rahab listed in the heroes of faith hall of fame.

> By faith the walls of Jericho fell down after they were encircled for seven days. By faith the harlot Rahab did not perish with those who did not believe, when she had received the spies with peace (Hebrews 11:30-31 NKJV).

The Samaritan Woman

This story begins with Jesus traveling to Galilee and intentionally making a detour to pass through a city of Samaria called Sychar. Being weary from His journey, He stopped at the well outside town around noon while His disciples went to buy food. A Samaritan woman comes by to draw water. Why at the hottest time of the day? She had her reasons. He says to her, "Give me some water to drink," surprising to her because Jews had nothing to do with Samaritans. "You are a Jew and You know Jews have no dealing with Samaritans," she says.

He ignores the question and engages her in a conversation that will cause her to open up. Now begins the first phase of unveiling who He is.

"If you knew the gift of God and that He that is speaking with you, you would know that He is the one now requesting of you a drink." He is really telling her, "If you would but ask of Me, I will give you the life-giving water you thirst for. I am the giver of this true life." Although He is speaking to her in spiritual terms, the eyes of her understanding have not been opened to the depth of His words. But slowly, with patience and grace, He gives her the opportunity to receive this new knowledge.

She responds to Him, "You have nothing to draw with, so how is it possible that You have this living water?" Her second question is "Who are You anyway? Are you greater than our father Jacob who gave us this well?" Jesus meets her first in the natural world, and uses that as a springboard for the spiritual encounter. He says, "He that drinks from this natural well will thirst again. It can only quench a natural thirst. However, I speak to you of something greater."

Now He carefully shows her a second revelation of who He is. "I am the giver of eternal life, both the author and principle of life. Whoever will drink of the water that I give them, My grace

The ReCreated Woman

will be made available. That person will never have the spiritual thirst that lies dormant and active in all of humanity. You see, I have come to fill this thirst." This is humankind's longing and profound need for God.

It is here that the eyes of her spiritual conscience are opened. She gains a spiritual thirst. She buys into this truth. She sees the benefit of it before she recognizes that behind her physical need is a hunger and thirst for righteousness and through Him she can be filled. He drives His point home further to meet her personal need and to identify her issue.

"Go and bring your husband back with you."

"I have no husband," she replies.

"In this you speak the truth, for you have had five husbands and the one you are with now is not your husband."

Now we can see the inner dialogue in her heart surfacing, "I now perceive You are a prophet, so I can converse with You about spiritual things. Our fathers worshiped in this mountain but the Jews made the place of worship Jerusalem, so who is right?" Here is the third revelation to her.

Jesus replied, "Even though you worship here, you do not know what it is you worship. We know what we worship for salvation comes from the Jews. The hour is coming and behold it is now upon you when true worship will spring forth from the heart. It will not be a physical place for worship. You do not know what you worship even though you say the place is here in the mountain." He is zooming in on her issue of concern. "The worship I speak of is in spirit and in truth. This is the kind of worship the Father seeks and is what is pleasing to Him. Worship must take place in the spirit because He is Spirit. The truth must be known and revealed for this true worship to take place in the hearts of men. This truth is what I came to reveal to humanity." We can see how carefully He guides her step by step so her understanding will become more enlightened.

She accepts His words and wants to know how she can receive the truth. "I know it will happen when the Messiah comes. I know He is on the way and I am patiently awaiting His arrival, for when He comes He will reveal all truth to me." Can you imagine all of this time she is literally speaking with the Messiah, the one she is waiting for while He is at that very moment revealing to her something she expects to take place in the future?

Now He reveals to her who He is: "I that speak with you am He."

The woman was so overjoyed she dropped her bucket and ran to the city to tell the people the good news. She herself went to witness to them the things she had seen and heard. Many believed on Him based on her words alone, the Bible says they went looking for Him and requested that He stay with them. He extended His stay by two days. And many more believed on Him now because of hearing the word directly from Him and came to their own revelation of Him. They knew without a doubt He is the Christ, the Savior of the world!

A woman despised by her people ignored that rejection to proclaim Jesus to them. She literally won a whole city to Christ based on that one encounter with Him.

Mary Magdalene

Who was the first person to proclaim the resurrection message? It was Mary Magdalene among a group of faithful women who had been with Jesus at the foot of the cross. She was the first to witness the empty tomb and went to tell the disciples. John and Peter followed and saw the empty tomb, but after they discovered the truth, they left. However, Mary lingered on.

This episode of the empty tomb and the encounter with Jesus is so important it is recorded in the four gospels. The fullest account here is from John 20:1-18 NKJV:

> Now the first *day* of the week Mary Magdalene went to the tomb early, while it was still dark, and saw *that* the stone had been taken away from the

tomb. ² Then she ran and came to Simon Peter, and to the other disciple, whom Jesus loved, and said to them, "They have taken away the Lord out of the tomb, and we do not know where they have laid Him."

³ Peter therefore went out, and the other disciple, and were going to the tomb. ⁴ So they both ran together, and the other disciple outran Peter and came to the tomb first. ⁵ And he, stooping down and looking in, saw the linen cloths lying *there;* yet he did not go in. ⁶ Then Simon Peter came, following him, and went into the tomb; and he saw the linen cloths lying *there,* ⁷ and the handkerchief that had been around His head, not lying with the linen cloths, but folded together in a place by itself. ⁸ Then the other disciple, who came to the tomb first, went in also; and he saw and believed. ⁹ For as yet they did not know the Scripture, that He must rise again from the dead. ¹⁰ Then the disciples went away again to their own homes.

¹¹ But Mary stood outside by the tomb weeping, and as she wept she stooped down *and looked* into the tomb. ¹² And she saw two angels in white

sitting, one at the head and the other at the feet, where the body of Jesus had lain. ¹³ Then they said to her, "Woman, why are you weeping?"

She said to them, "Because they have taken away my Lord, and I do not know where they have laid Him."

¹⁴ Now when she had said this, she turned around and saw Jesus standing *there*, and did not know that it was Jesus. ¹⁵ Jesus said to her, "Woman, why are you weeping? Whom are you seeking?"

She, supposing Him to be the gardener, said to Him, "Sir, if You have carried Him away, tell me where You have laid Him, and I will take Him away."

¹⁶ Jesus said to her, "Mary!"

She turned and said to Him, "Rabboni!" (which is to say, Teacher).

¹⁷ Jesus said to her, "Do not cling to Me, for I have not yet ascended to My Father; but go to My brethren and say to them, 'I am ascending to

My Father and your Father, and *to* My God and your God.'"

¹⁸ Mary Magdalene came and told the disciples that she had seen the Lord, and *that* He had spoken these things to her.

Immediately as Mary Magdalene turned, she saw Jesus even if she did not know who He was. Jesus asked her the same question as the angels before, "Why are you weeping? Who is it that you seek?" Supposing Him to be the caretaker of the garden, she responds, "Where did you take Him? Where did you put Him? I will come personally and I will take Him away.

Can you imagine her desperation, clinging on to the last vestige of Him, His lifeless body? I know that the events had already been written in God's plan, but I am certain that Jesus just could not bear to hear her cries anymore. He had to reveal Himself to such a desperate seeker of Him. He called her name with tenderness and compassion, "Mary!" At this point she recognized His voice and was seized by such a sense of relief and turned to embrace Him.

Jesus said, "Hold on, do not touch Me, I have not ascended. I have not yet completed my assignment. I heard your weeping and your heartfelt cry and I stopped by to let you know I am alive and well. Go and tell my brethren the veil is rent and you now have access to the Father Himself."

Later that day, Jesus appeared to the two disciples on the road to Emmaus and then after that to the disciples as they gathered together in Jerusalem (Luke 24:13-53). Mary was the first evangelist of His resurrection. Blessed are the feet that bring good news!

What is significant about Jesus choosing Mary Magdalene as the first witness of His resurrection? Why did He appear to a woman and not to one of the disciples like Peter the leader or John the disciple whom He loved? And why was her name mentioned twelve times in the Gospels, more than most of the apostles?

I believe there are two important reasons. The first was the lowly stature of women in Jewish society at that time. Seen as uneducated and emotional, they were not considered credible witnesses in the eyes of the law. We see this when the women first witnessed to the disciples about the empty tomb, because Luke 24:11 says that "And their words seemed to them like idle tales, and they did not believe them." All but Peter and John remained in the house. But on finding the women were right, they themselves did not pursue the matter. Did God have a message about not appealing to our senses and preconceptions when exercising our faith?

The second reason was Mary Magdalene's background. Yes, she was an ardent follower of Jesus but she had a past. Many people believe she was a person of ill repute. The Bible makes no mention of that; instead, it reveals that she had been delivered by Jesus of seven demons.

> Jesus traveled about from one town and village to another, proclaiming the good news of the kingdom of God. The twelve were with him, and also some women who had been cured of evil spirits and diseases: Mary (called Magdalene) from whom seven demons had come out ... (Luke 8:1-2 NIV; also Mark 16:9),

Can you imagine what it must have been like for Mary to be exposed to the shame and reproach of her society by being linked to mental illness and demonic possession? This was reason enough for Jesus to shun her and not be in close proximity to a woman of such repute. But they didn't know Jesus. Such is the compassion of God for the weak and despised that He will make them His key witnesses. He will exonerate and exalt them, and put to shame the wisdom of the wise (1 Corinthians 1:27).

If we allow God to complete the work He desires in us, He will re-present us to the world and to ourselves as the woman He wants us to become. We are the Re-Created Woman, daughters of Father God, beloved of Him, fashioned for His purpose, and filled with His gifts, the most cherished being the gift of His Son, access to the Father and the precious gift of the Holy Spirit. He desires to bring us to the place of completeness in Him, fearfully and wonderfully made in Him. Rahab and the Woman of Samaria acted on what was revealed to them and this caused them both to reverse the course of their life. Now they had purpose, and knew the path towards their destiny, and newness of life for themselves, their family and an entire city and nation.

Receive the Peace

The peace of God is not limited to our pleasant moments in this life. It's a peace Jesus said that prevails over everything and lasts forever. "The peace I give no man can take it away. The world cannot take it away and neither will it diminish because of what you go through in this life." If we do not have this kind of peace, we must ask ourselves what we have traded it for. Worry, fear, quick fixes or denial of God's promises? Once we bring our thought life back to Jesus, our peace will return. We must walk in purity before God. We can do this if we give up the craving and lust for the things of this world that keep us bound to unhealthy and toxic relationships with no future. This keeps us compromising our values and godly morals.

We must love our bodies more than these things. I am not saying there's anything wrong with having natural desires but how we can sometimes go about satisfying them makes it wrong. We desire the right thing but go about getting it the wrong way. Even in our dress, we have to reprogram our minds to make sure we wear the proper attire that it is worn for the right reasons.

Sin lies in the intention just as much as the deed. It is okay to have nice things; however, to want them to be seen or to attract a certain kind of attention is wrong.

Hannah showed us how to respond to barriers. She was not allowed in the temple but she made for herself a temple outside the door of the temple (1 Samuel 2:1-10). The Shunammite woman who built a room for Elisha in her house showed us what to do when the miracle son promised by God died. She showed us how to show deference to a true man of God so that he does not become so familiar or common we lose our faith that he is able to resurrect the dead (see 2 Kings 4:8-37 and 2 Kings 8:1-6). Abigail showed us how to respect a king, and soothe a man in the heat of his anger (1 Samuel 25). Lydia, the trader of purple dye in the city of Thyatira, showed us how to accommodate Paul, the apostle with grace, dignity and character, and become a person of influence in spreading the gospel (Acts 16). The woman who broke the alabaster box showed us how to worship Jesus in public, regardless of the scorn in the eyes of the company. She that was forgiven much also loved much. All that mattered was that she was received in His company to wash His feet with her tears (Matthew 26:6-13).

The question now to you, my sister, becomes, "Will you be made whole? Will you empty yourself out to receive all that is required for wholeness?"

He is asking, "Can I make you whole? All that I did for others like you, can I now do for you? Will you allow Me to be a reality in your life? Can I give you this gift to saturate you and take you over totally?"

This is where the rubber meets the road in your life. This is the defining moment. Will you choose the new way – His way – or continue in the entrapment of the past life, the life you have been freed from?

If you take the journey with Him, all stakes are on Him as long as you go in faith and obedience. You have nothing to lose and all to gain. You must trust Him enough to confront the fears, the disappointments and the heartbreaks buried in your life. Trust and rely on Him. He knows exactly what this life should look like for each one of us. All He is concerned with is to care for and keep us under His wing. Absolute trust in Him will mean you are committed to letting go of the weight that hinders you, and pressing forward toward the goal in Christ Jesus.

To every woman reading this book, here are the standards of a godly man. If you are wondering how you will recognize him when he comes, or if you missed him, you would know based on the characteristics in the Commitment Pledge at the end.

If you are single, then make a covenant with Father God to keep yourself pure until He sends this kind of man to find you. While you are waiting, make a commitment to allow God to complete the work in you to be the gift He desires you to become for this man and, more so, for His glory. We must take on a higher standard with morals to purposely have values. Never forget, God made you to complement the man, not inferior, but suitable, adaptable, to have dominion and to govern all given to him by God. This is what God saw fit to require as a need for your man to fulfill the whole of the command and to be fruitful, multiply and replenish the earth. You are secure from having to compete with ungodly appetites in men for acceptance because you are made in His image and in His likeness. Will you take the pledge to enter into a covenant with Father God to wait until this man has found you?

If you are married, then take what you have gained and go into your prayer closet and stay there until God makes him this man for you. Use the words below as your prayer guide and design for the man you desire.

Commitment Pledge

To the man,

The man of whom I am his rib ... to this
man I am more than enough.

This man is like Boaz. He will not settle down until He
has put his affairs in order for me to become his wife.

This man knows how to love and to minister
to me, and he gives and reserves himself, as
Christ did for His church, only to me.

To this man, intimacy is a sacred ministry exchanged and
given only to me, and only in the covenant of marriage.

He is sensitive to me both in the natural and in the spirit.

He understands his first ministry is to me as unto the Lord.
This is the covenant of marriage instituted by God.

He understands this and his role to leave and to cleave, to cover, to protect and to provide. This man bears the responsibility for the completion of each role in obedience to God.

He values the trust and the respect I give and he holds this as a treasure; he will seek no opportunity to destroy it.

There is no need to accept or to compete with the spirit of pride, seducing spirits, or the spirit of lust.

God formed and fashioned me as His gift for the right man. I am made in His image and His likeness.

This man knows who he is in God and he operates and governs himself accordingly. Upholding godly standards, godly character and principles, he sets biblical boundaries for his life and character.

To this man, I am more than enough ...
I am what completes him – his missing rib.

Name: _____ Date: _____

Notes

Merriam-Webster: America's Most Trusted Dictionary

Oxford Dictionary

Wikipedia

Dakes Annotated Reference Bible The Old and New Testament, with notes, Concordance and Index @ Copyright holders Melanie Dake, Edward Finnis Dake, Monique Germaine, Kimberly Dake Kennedy, Kathryn Dake Iglinksi and Dake Ministries Lawrenceville, Georgia KJV Edition @ Copyright 2014 Fifth Printing – December 2019

Matthew Henry's Commentary On The Whole Bible New modern addition Complete and Unabridged in Six Volumes Copyright @ 1991 by Hendrickson Publishers, Inc. Seventh Printing – January 2003

https://bibletools.org

Notes

Books by
Tabitha Henton Lamb

Contending For The Faith
The Battleground of the Mind

God's Relationship With Man

Strengthening Your Faith
A Toolkit for the Believers

The Surrendered Life
A Pearl of Immense Value

Weathering Life's Storms
Equipping Yourself to Face the Challenges

Understanding God's Plan
Re-evaluating Your Relationship With God

The Purpose of Pain
How God Uses Pain to Strengthen Your Resolve

Enriching the Immortal Soul
A Journey Towards God

Available wherever online books are sold.

Author Contact Information

You may contact the author at:

2008 Airline Drive, Ste. 300 #202

Bossier City, LA 71111

Email: admin@thlministries.org

www.thlministries.org

phone: 318-918-9248

Made in the USA
Monee, IL
15 October 2024

68011752R00066